DATING

FOR

DUMMIES®

D0126192

A Running Press Miniature Edition™
Copyright © 1997, IDG Books Worldwide, Inc.

Library of Congress Cataloging-in-Publication Number
99-70303
ISBN 0-7624-0631-3

This book may be ordered by mail from the publisher.
Please add $1.00 for postage and handling.
But try your bookstore first!

Running Press Book Publishers
125 South Twenty-second Street
Philadelphia, Pennsylvania 19103-4399

Log onto www.specialfavors.com to order Running Press
Miniature Editions™ with your own custom-made covers!

Visit us on the web!
www.runningpress.com

Miniature Editions™

DATING

FOR

DUMMIES®

A Reference
for the Rest of Us!™

by Dr. Joy Browne

RUNNING PRESS
PHILADELPHIA · LONDON

Icons used in this book

 This icon marks general information that is important enough for you to keep in mind.

 This icon indicates information that is detrimental to you, your date, or your dating experience.

 Periodically, there are points that I think you need to pay special attention to, for your own well-being and best interest.

Contents

The 5th Wave® By Rich Tennant

@RICHTENNANT

"I'm looking for someone who will love me for who I think I am."

Introduction

Dating makes everybody feel like a dummy. Why such sweaty palms if men and women have been getting together for thousands of years? It's because the rules have all changed. Adam and Eve were the original blind date and it's been a lot rockier ever since.

Before you find yourself

hyperventilating, remember that there is no single, right way to date or to ask somebody out. And there is no such thing as a perfect experience that will make someone fall madly and passionately in love with you. A date is unique in every situation.

But not to worry: This book helps you get it all sorted out so that you can feel like you know what

you're doing, have some
sense of direction and some
idea of what your date is
doing and thinking, and
even have some fun.

 Remember, the nice
thing about a date is
that it's just a date.

Chapter 1

. . . .

Predate Warmups

The Confidence Game

Confidence is the ability to trust yourself and convey that sense to others, and appearance is half the battle. To appear confident try the following:

- ✔ Stand up straight.
- ✔ Smile.
- ✔ Make eye contact.
- ✔ Lean slightly forward.
- ✔ Shake hands firmly.

You're ready to date if

- ✔ You've got a stable place to live and a way to make a living.
- ✔ You have a reasonably good working relationship with your parents (a cease fire is good enough).
- ✔ You have a friend or two hanging about.
- ✔ You know how to make yourself reasonably happy.
- ✔ You'd really like some

tension and aggravation and excitement and fun and worry and uncertainty in your life.

The Best Places to Meet People Are Ones in Which

- ✔ You can see clearly, hear clearly, and respond honestly.
- ✔ You have an interest in what's going on, increasing the likelihood you'll

have something in common with anyone you meet there.

✔ The atmosphere feels safe and familiar.

Where to meet people

✔ **The classroom:** High schools, colleges, and adult education classes are all dating mills.

✔ **Parties:** Meeting someone at a party offers one of the same advantages that meeting someone in your neighborhood offers: You both know somebody in common.

✔ **Movies:** The line into the movie, especially if it's a long line, is not a bad place to get to know somebody.

✔ **Dances:** Folk dancing is great, as is square dancing, because the caller tells you what to do, and you're always changing partners.

▶ **Grocery stores:** Buying
food in the local market
has that comfort/familiar-
ity/nurturing thing going.
It's a (usually) non-threat-
ening environment,
you've probably been
there before, and if no
one datable happens to
meander in front of your
grocery cart or pause
invitingly in the produce
section, you can still pick

up your milk and Ding-
Dongs.

- **Bus stops:** Waiting at the
same place and at the
same time every day
creates a sense of commu-
nity. You see each other—
and every other regular
passenger—here all the
time, and you can sit
together. The trick here is to
go slowly (pun intended).

- **Laundromats:** What's
more domestic than

airing your once dirty, now clean, laundry in public? Always carry extra fabric softener and change (you never know who may need to borrow something), and under no circumstances mention underwear.

- **Bookstores:** Some chains have actually put in big, old comfy chairs and jazz quartets. Spending time in one of these bookstores is sort of like hanging out at the library except that you're allowed to talk, drink coffee, and compare notes.

✔ **Restaurants:** Asking to join someone sitting alone is a bit iffy. If the person says yes, it saves you from eating alone, but if they say no, you may lose your appetite.

✔ **Church:** Many churches and synagogues have special singles' services and events, figuring it's safe and familiar and spiritual, and with any luck at all, increases the wedding business.

✓ **Volunteer activities:** Being your most altruistic self is hard to resist, and having something in common with another altruistic soul gives you lots to talk about. Just make sure that you like the activity itself. After all, you don't want to end up licking envelopes to save sperm whales because you heard fishermen have great poles.

✔ **Political campaigns:** Political campaigns offer a nearly perfect environment because there's a common goal, it doesn't go on forever, and the atmosphere is exciting and intense.

✔ **Sport teams:** Even if

you're a klutz, find a sport to play. It's safe, it's fun, it's physical, and there are almost always some sort of get-togethers afterwards—especially if you win.

✔ **Sporting events:** Most people are really relaxed when they watch sports—unless it's the playoffs—and they are quite willing to explain what's going on or to argue about who's best. So asking the cute person next to you, "What's the score?" will likely get you a smile rather than a slap.

✔ **Health clubs:** Health clubs have a lot going for them: You're among other people doing essentially the same thing you are. You probably see the same group of people all the time and are, therefore, familiar with them.

Keep in mind, though, that everybody is in span-dex and therefore often a bit shy.

Where NOT to meet people

✔ **The office:** Everybody will know about it and one of you will very likely get fired. Work is about competence, and any-thing that interferes with that is poison. It may be tempting to date friends, sibs, or exes of people you work with, but it's still not very safe, so don't, at least unless you plan to change jobs—voluntarily.

- **Bars:** It's dark, most everybody has been ingesting substances that alter perception, and who needs a relationship based on blurred sensibilities? Plus, bars are too noisy to talk in, and you can't see what the person looks like. If nothing else, how do you answer "Come here often?"

✔ **Online:** Online is about fantasy. It's the illusion of intimacy while still being at arm's length. When you do meet face to face, there is all that expectation. It's okay to chat, but online is the ultimate long distance relationship. You'll think you know much more than you really know, and that's really tricky.

- ✔ **Singles dances:** The air of desperation is palpable, but if you can go and have fun, you'll probably do okay, 'cause you'll stand out as the only person really having a good time.

- ✔ **Singles weekends:** These weekends mean too much stress and too high expectations. You're better off spending the same money and taking a cruise; at least that way you can feel your money is well spent even if you don't fall in love.

Expectations Worksheet

*Start by listing all
the qualities your ideal
date absolutely, posi-
tively must have.*

My date must be:

1. _____
2. _____
3. _____
4. _____

Now, list all the qualities your ideal date absolutely, positively must not have.

My date must NOT be:

1. _____
2. _____
3. _____
4. _____

Chapter 2

. . . .

Setting Up
the Date

When You Approach Someone, Take This Advice

✔ **Be sincere:** The key to being sincere is to mean what you say. Pleeeeze don't practice sincerity in front of the mirror. For sincerity to work, you have to focus on the object (person, please) of your desire and believe what you are saying.

✔ **Be honest:** If you're a
rotten dancer, say in a
self-effacing, engaging
way that you have two
left feet. Don't try to
make yourself someone
you're not to impress
someone you may or may
not like. Don't pretend
to love jazz, collect
Porsches, or own a yacht.
On the other hand, telling
the truth isn't the same
as baring your soul.

✔ **Be friendly:** When you're friendly, you smile, you're open, you're fun to be around.

✔ **Be positive:** I'm not talking goody-two-shoes here, just pleasant and upbeat.

Pick-up Lines

Don't even think about using lines like these:

✔ "Come here often?"
✔ "What's your sign?"

✔ "I must have died and gone to heaven because where else would I see an angel like you?"

✔ "If I tell you that you have a beautiful body, would you hold it against me?"

So rather than practicing a pick-up line, follow these two guidelines:

Focus on the situation and your feelings. "I couldn't help myself; I just had to come over and tell you your smile was keeping me from concentrating," is ever so much better than "Are you new around here?"

If the line sounds like a title to a country song, don't use it.

A Word on Compliments

It's okay to compliment men on their

- ✔ **Hair:** Thick, shiny, wavy, healthy locks, nice cut, attractive color. But don't talk about receding hairlines, bald spots, early graying, or dandruff.
- ✔ **Eyes:** Everyone loves to hear that they've got nice eyes. Try adjectives like warm and expressive.
- ✔ **Neck:** If he's got a neck like a wrestler, tell him. If it's a chicken neck, let it pass.

- **Clothing:** Tie—cut, color, style. But don't say you want to use it to tie him to a bedpost—at least not yet. Socks—some men take a lot of care picking their socks. Stun—and impress—him by noticing, but never lift his pant leg without asking.
- **Smile:** Men love to hear that they've got a charming, handsome, alluring smile.

Women find it cool to be praised for essentially the same things

- ✔ **Hair:** Women spend a lot of time on their hair, and they like the effort noticed. But don't touch without asking, be careful about noting an unusual color (two out of three women in America color their hair), and never say "dye."
- ✔ **Eyes:** Like I said before,

everyone likes to be complimented on their eyes.

✔ **Neck:** Complimenting a woman on her neck can often be a bit iffy—unless it's long and slender.

✔ **Smile:** Women love to hear that they've got a warm, engaging, sweet smile.

Asking for a Date

Face it, the only thing scarier

than the first date is asking
for the first date. But if you
can remember that you're not
looking for a cure for cancer,
that you won't die even if
they say yes, and that life as
we know it will continue no
matter what they say, it may
help you to ask.

Asking dos and don'ts

Never ask for a first
date for a Friday or
Saturday night. Start

off with a Wednesday or a Thursday instead.

Never say, "Would you like to go out sometime?" Instead, be specific.

Always offer options about the date. If your potential date doesn't like the suggested activity but does like you, you can modify your plan.

Remember that timing is everything. A basic rule is to ask for a first date a week to ten days in advance.

"You're a great geek, Martin. You're just not my geek."

Planning a Date:

A first date can be ulcer material; to make yours as comfortable as possible, follow these ten basic rules:

1. Pick an activity that you enjoy.

2. Pick an activity that you can easily afford.

3. Do something that doesn't require new clothes.

4. Go where you can talk without getting thrown out.

5. Go to a place that's easy to get to.

6. Do something that isn't competitive.

7. Pick an activity that doesn't involve a lot of alcohol.

8. Leave time to get to know each other.

9. Do something that doesn't involve others.

10. Find an activity that doesn't last more than a couple of hours.

Good Places for a First Date

- ✔ **Museums:** At a museum, you get to meander through the halls, look at exhibits, and chat about anything that inspires you. It's a great place to get to know each other and to see each other's tastes in art—or whatever. Overall, a museum is relaxed, easy, and inexpensive.

✔ **Amusement parks:**
Unless it's really hard to
get to, going to an amusement park is usually fun
and makes everybody
feel young and carefree.
The only real problems?
Sticky fingers from cotton
candy and rides that
make you so queasy
you'd give up your first
born for an antacid
tablet, but all in all, a
good choice.

- **Walks:** You can take walks (almost) anywhere: parks, zoos, botanical gardens, and so on. It's cheap, fun, and pressure-free. Plus, you can often hold hands.

- **Outdoor activities in general:** Sporting events, concerts, and picnics are great places for first dates. You can talk, and being outside, everything feels less claustrophobic.

First dates to avoid

- ✔ Weddings.
- ✔ New Year's Eve parties.
- ✔ Valentine's Day.
- ✔ Thanksgiving dinner.

Chapter 3

· ·

The Date

Emergency Repair Kit:

Hey, life happens. But that doesn't mean you can't be ready for any eventuality. Keep a shoe box handy and full of the following stuff:

- Safety pins.
- Needle and thread.
- Styptic pencil (men and women).
- Extra pair of pantyhose.
- Band-Aids.

✔ Clear nail polish.
✔ Hem tape.
✔ Tweezers.
✔ Antacid tablets.
✔ Breath mints.

D-day Hygiene Checklist

To make sure you covered all the bases, follow this D-day hygiene checklist:

✔ Shower.
✔ Hair washed.

- ✔ Ears washed (inside, out, and behind).
- ✔ Teeth brushed/flossed.
- ✔ Nails clipped/filed (don't forget your toenails—hey, you never know).
- ✔ Shave (face, legs, armpits).
- ✔ Pluck (guys: pay special attention to the bridge of your nose and earlobes; women: don't skip the chiny chin chin).
- ✔ Deodorant (go for the

gold; use an antiperspirant).
- ✔ Clean underwear (mom
  was right again).
- ✔ Freshly laundered clothes.

One Final Checklist

- ✔ Know where you're going.
- ✔ Know how to get there.
- ✔ Make sure you have
  enough gas.
- ✔ Know how much (more
  or less) thing are going
  to cost.

- ✔ Make sure you have enough money.
- ✔ Make sure you have $20 tucked somewhere for emergencies.
- ✔ Make sure your watch is working.

Also check the following:

- ✔ Breath.
- ✔ Teeth.
- ✔ Wallet.
- ✔ Pits.
- ✔ Wardrobe.

- ✔ Baby-sitter (when appropriate).
- ✔ Curfew (when appropriate).
- ✔ Calendar.
- ✔ Date's phone number.
- ✔ Date's address.
- ✔ Tickets (for time and date).

Money

 The time to swing by the ATM machine is the day before your date. Nothing kills the illusion of a together, take-charge person faster than fumbling with your PIN number while your date waits in the car. Don't assume the place you're going takes credit cards. If you don't know, bring enough cash to cover the most expensive item on the menu or at the venue.

Who pays?

Follow this two-part rule:

1. If you ask, you pay. This ensures that whoever does the inviting knows what things will cost and has budgeted accordingly. If you can't afford the activity, scale down and do something else.

2. The other person offers but doesn't insist on helping out. No empty gestures, please. And no fights to the death. It's charming to offer, but don't push it, and be willing to treat next time.

Tipping

Have a few dollar bills handy for tipping valets, and so on. For a rough estimate on how much you'll need for tips, use the following guide:

Waiters/waitresses: 15 to 20 percent of total bill
Cab drivers: 15 to 20 percent of fare (but never less than $1)
Valet parkers: $2
Coat check: $1 per coat
Restroom attendant: $1

Say What?

Opening parlay

Icebreakers are designed to put both you and your date at ease. Some good opening gambits include:

- ✔ What did you do today? (shows interest and presumably everyone did something).
- ✔ What book (movie, TV show, and so on) is your favorite?

✔ Are you a cat or a dog person?

Safe subjects

Create a conversational comfort zone with tidbits designed to put both you and your date at ease that include:

✔ **Weather:** The old chestnut, "Nice weather we're having," is a waste. But confiding that the sky was so clear and beautiful

you spent your lunch
hour barefoot in the park
is another story entirely.
- **Location:** Where you
  are right now is a great
  subject for conversation.
  Commenting on the
  colors, smells, sounds,
  and tastes in a positive
  way (no griping allowed)
  allows you to share
  the experience.
- **Friends in common:**
  Beware of gossip, but

establishing links is a very good idea.

- ✔ **News events:** Be up to date, read the paper or a news magazine.
- ✔ **Popular culture:** Talk about plays, movies, concerts, rock stars, and so on.

Taboo topics

- ✔ Sex.
- ✔ Ex.
- ✔ Politics.
- ✔ Religion.

Foods to Fear on a First Date

Stay away from these foods
unless you have breath mints,
dental floss, and guts:

- Garlic.
- Corn on the cob.
- Poppy seeds.
- Popcorn.
- Whole lobster.
- French onion soup.
- Ribs.
- Fried chicken.

- ✔ Watermelon.

The Kiss Question

You can tell that a woman is interested in a kiss if:

- ✔ She's facing you, arms down, body relaxed.
- ✔ Her head is tilted upward.
- ✔ She doesn't appear to be ending the date with some definitive remark like, "Thanks. I'll call you."
- ✔ Her lips are parted.

▪ ✔ She gazes into your eyes.

If she's not interested, she'll:
- ✔ Clamp her jaw shut.
- ✔ Fumble for her keys.
- ✔ Refuse to look you in the eye.
- ✔ Glue her chin to her chest.
- ✔ Hold out her hand and say, "Thanks."

You can tell a guy is looking forward to a little lip action because he will:

- ✔ Position his body between you and the door.
- ✔ Act nervous.
- ✔ Show no visible signs of leaving or ending the date.
- ✔ Tilt his head upward.
- ✔ Lick his lips.

If he's not interested, he'll:

- ✔ Walk you directly to your door or car, without hesitation.
- ✔ Keep his hands in his pockets.

✔ Look at his feet.
✔ Avoid eye contact at
   all costs.

How to Kiss

Though there is no "right"
way to kiss, here are a few
pointers to help you success-
fully land a lip-lock:

✔ **Check out your date's
   body language:** See pre-
   vious section for signs.
✔ **As soon as you decide to**

go for it, do it: Hovering near some girl's or guy's lips will only make both of you freak out.

✔ **Maintain eye contact on the way to your date's lips:** Don't shut your eyes until you arrive, or you may get lost on the way.

✔ **Start gently:** Press your lips sweetly against your date's. Save the tongue action for later.

✔ **Pull back:** Gaze into your

date's eyes. If it's a go, you'll know by the way he or she looks longingly back at you. If not, smile and say goodnight and your face will be nicely saved.

The second lip-press is when you can go French: This means tongue. This doesn't mean gagging your date or thrusting home or swallowing his or her tongue as soon as it darts into your mouth. Instead, gingerly part your lips and venture forth.

✔ **A light, flickering touch with your tongue can produce major results:** The tongue is a cluster of nerve-endings. Imagine "caressing" your date's tongue and lips and mouth.

✔ **Don't overdo it:** Variety—kissing the eye-

lashes, neck, nibbling
on the lips—is the
spice that flavors all
great kissing.

How to Survive Dating's Most Embarrassing Moments

Your pants (skirt, shirt, or bra) split.
Tie your jacket or sweater around your waist; buy or borrow a jacket or sweater to

tie around your waist; borrow
a safety pin from the waiter.

**You forgot your wallet or
billfold.**

*Throw yourself on the mercy
of either your date or the man-
ager (if you're a regular there).
If your date likes you, at least
he or she will know there
will be another date—one
for which you pay in full.*

You get sick.

*Hey, sick happens. Just don't
deny it so long that you get*

sick right then and there. Tell your date you're not feeling well and need a few minutes in the restroom. If you really don't think you're going to make it, ask your date for help. Passing out in a bathroom stall will only make a bad situation worse. It's okay to ask for a rain check— or a barf check or a nasal drip check.

You pass wind.

Most importantly, avoid break-

ing out in a 15-minute nervous laughing jag. Apologize once and then (if possible) open a window.

You run into an angry ex.

Remind yourself that you are not responsible for anyone's behavior but your own. Stay calm and let your ex be the only person in the room who makes a fool of him or herself.

Your car breaks down.

Presumably you belong to an auto club so you won't have to

*flip through the yellow pages
looking for a reputable tow.
Don't get frustrated. Best thing
to do is make the best of it.
See whether the tow truck can
drop you off at the restaurant
on the way, take a cab home,
and deal with your dead
car tomorrow.*

 Remember, a little
reconnaissance
means you won't
run out of gas or get a flat
without a spare.

Ten Keys to a Happy and Rewarding Dating Experience

1. Be realistic.
2. Be specific.
3. Take responsibility.
4. Be active.
5. Don't settle.
6. Evaluate often.
7. Write stuff down.
8. Be creative.
9. Be aware.
10. Analyze fear.

The 5th Wave® By Rich Tennant

"I don't know, Mona—sometimes I get the feeling you're afraid to get close."

Disaster Dates

What to do when you hate your date

- ✔ Be polite.
- ✔ Stay put.
- ✔ Have a conversation.
- ✔ Listen.
- ✔ See your date home.
- ✔ Behave as you'd like to be treated.

Using tact

Here's a list of some tactful

translations for how you may really feel:

I want to go home now.

Translation: *Gee, it sure is getting late, and I've got an early morning tomorrow.*

You bore me to tears.

Translation: *Please excuse my yawning; it's been a really tough week.*

We have nothing in common.

Translation: *You've led such a different life than I have!*

You sure seemed nicer

when I asked you out.

Translation: *There are so many sides to your personality.*

What a waste of time!

Translation: *I've been in such a time crunch these days, I never have time for the fun stuff.*

You look nothing like your picture.

Translation: *Your photo doesn't do you justice.*

Why don't you say something instead of just sitting there?

Translation: *You seem quiet—
are you okay?*

Are you ever going to shut up?

Translation: *You're so full
of energy!*

I never want to see you again.

Translation: *Tonight has been
an experience. Thank you.*

Date Pathology 101 Worksheet

Fill out this worksheet as soon as you can after the date ends, when your impressions are still fresh.

Your Date's Name _____

How you met _____

Date, Time, Place: _____

_____

Rating (0 – 10) _____

Signs and Symptoms

Make sure you're being
really specific here (for
example, nice smile,
when we met, good table
manners, well-groomed).

Positive stuff _____
_____

Icky poo poo stuff _____
_____

Chapter 4

. . . .

The Day After
and Beyond

The Next Day

Five ways to put a hideous date in perspective

1. Rent *Fatal Attraction*.

2. Thank technology for VCRs—you didn't have to miss anything while you were out.

3. Count how many days you've been alive. Subtract only one.

4. Look at your watch—it just seemed like forever.

5. Check your pulse. You survived!

Anatomy of a True Second Date

A Second Date Is

- ✔ A next step.
- ✔ A continued search for compatibility.
- ✔ A time to flirt.
- ✔ A chance to reveal yourself.
- ✔ A shift of focus onto your date.

A Second Date Isn't

- ✔ A relationship.
- ✔ A pre-spouse interview.

- ✔ A confessional.
- ✔ A time to have sex.
- ✔ Obsessing about yourself.

The beauty of a second date is that real personalities can begin to emerge.

Casual versus Serious versus Heavy Dating

Casual dating
Casual dating means that

neither of you is taking the relationship terribly seriously because one or the other of you is:

- ✔ **Dating others:** You like each other but see other people as well.
- ✔ **Living far away from each other:** You can only see each other occasionally.
- ✔ **Only in town temporarily:** You know that the relationship will last only as long

as the business trip, vacation, or whatever does.

- ✔ **Not interested in a commitment:** You want the relationship to be without long-term expectations.
- ✔ **Not being sexual:** You're abstaining.
- ✔ **Not being seriously sexual:** You're not being monogamous (not a terrific idea).

Casual dating has much to recommend it: It allows

both parties to get to know
one another without the pres-
sure of exclusivity, and it
allows for comparisons that
are natural and not necessarily
odious.

Serious dating

Serious dating is a transition
between casual dating and
heavy dating:

- ✔ Your relationship is ex-
  clusive.
- ✔ You see each other once

or twice a week.

✔ You live in the same city.

✔ You are possibly sexual, possibly not.

DR. JOY SAYS The idea of dating is to see who's out there and to keep dosey-doeing and switching off until you find someone who seems a cut above the rest, someone worthy of additional time and effort and consideration. Once you

decide that you have someone who is worth abandoning
all others for—at least temporarily—you've moved
into exclusivity, which is a
precursor to heavy dating.

Heavy dating

Heavy dating has these
characteristics:

- ✓ **Mutual exclusivity by
  design:** You discuss and
  consciously agree to see
  only one another.

- ✔ **Having three or more dates a week:** You take time and effort to be together often.
- ✔ **Weekend dating:** You spend weekends together, rather than out with the guys or girls, and, when you do have to be with others, you often go as a couple.
- ✔ **Living in the same area code:** Living relatively close to one another

makes it possible to see each other often.

- ✔ **Often implies sex and certainly sexual exclusivity:** In other words, if your relationship includes sex, you are monogamous.

- ✔ **Sexual intimacy:** Although not necessary to a committed relationship, it is often one of its hallmarks. Whereas some think the key is the "sex" part, the real key is the "intimacy" part. If you think that you can achieve intimacy solely through sex, you're mistaken.

Like versus Lust versus Love

Diana Ross was right: You can't hurry love. You just have to wait. True love is a slow-burn. No two ways about it.

✔ **Like:** When you like someone, you're still in checklist mode. You're keeping a mental score-board—plus one for showing up on time, minus one for taking a call on the car's cell phone, plus one for laughing at your dumb joke, minus one for biting fingernails. "Like" is an evaluation of compati-bility—literally, seeing if

you two are enough
alike to get along.

- ✔ **Lust:** More physical than
  mental, lust is tingling
  fingertips, sweaty palms,
  pounding hearts, and
  breathless kisses. Lust is
  wanting to engulf some-
  one with a bear hug and
  make out (or more) 'til
  the sun comes up. Lust is
  powerful and fickle. It's a
  sexual faucet that can
  seem to turn off almost

as quickly as it turns
on—pure energy.

> **Lust with direction:**
After date two, before
date twenty-two, the LWD
phase is sexy with street
smarts. You've lost your
head over this person but
not your mind. Not only
do you desire to whisk
them off to bed in a cas-
cade of kisses, but you
want to read the morning
paper together, too. And

not just the funny pages, either.

- ✓ **Love:** Soft-focus in the best sense of the word. Most of all, love is about trust and time—and the time it takes to really trust someone fully. Love isn't a mad dash; it's a slow stroll. It's compatibility, acceptance, giving as well as getting, warmth, fun, and shared interests and goals. It's caring for someone, not in spite of their flaws, but because of them.

Ten ways to know you're in love

1. You actually want to meet the parents.

2. You're willing to explain why you don't want to date others.

3. You'll ditch your little black book.

4. You breathe easier when

he/she is around.

5. You hum love songs under your breath.

6. You're full of energy.

7. You're willing to go somewhere you hate.

8. You're willing to save if you're a spendthrift and spend if you're chintzy.

9. The idea of doing nothing together sounds terrific.

10. You're willing to risk being yourself.

Yep, looks like love to me!

When to say "I love you" (and when to keep quiet)

Few things are more memorable than the magical, angst-ridden, fingers-crossed, breath-held, passion-filled moment when either you or your date says, "I love you." It's much more than three little words. It's also a silent question. As in, "Do you love me, too?" Properly managing this moment can spell the difference between euphoria and humiliation.

Tips:

- ✒ Wait at least several months, a minimum of three, but preferably longer, before confessing your true love—even if you feel it on the first night. It takes a while to gain and build trust. Zooming ahead too fast can easily backfire, and it's really embarrassing

to find out you changed
your mind and you don't
really love 'em.

✔ If your date says, "I love
you" and you don't love
your date back, don't say,
"Love you, too" just to be
nice. You'll open a can of
worms that'll only make
a gigantic mess.

✔ If you've been together
a while and you're just
waiting for your date to
spill the beans first, take

a chance and tell him or her how you feel. Your date may be waiting for you to take the plunge.

✔ Realize that "love" doesn't always mean the same thing to everyone. For some, the word "love" is followed by the word "marriage." For others, "love" is always followed by "ya." Make sure you're clear on how you feel before putting your feel-

ings into words and give
a thought to the way your
date might receive what
you're about to say.

✔ Understand that true
love implies commitment.
If you're not ready to be
monogamous, connected,
open, and loving, don't
say "I love you" just yet.

✔ If the only time you're
tempted to confess love
is during sex or when
you're apart, close your

mouth, open your eyes, and see what's really going on.

Ending a Relationship

The warning signs:

- ✔ You fight over nothing.
- ✔ You're not as affectionate.
- ✔ You don't see what you ever saw in this person.
- ✔ You decided all your friends were right and have been all along.

- ✔ Your parents absolutely adore your date and that really frosts you.
- ✔ If there was ever sex, it has stopped.
- ✔ More time passes between dates.
- ✔ There are longer and longer silences.
- ✔ You start mentally (and maybe verbally, but I hope not) comparing your date unfavorably to others.

- You are more tempted by others.
- You're looking for excuses to be alone.
- You're looking for excuses to hang out with other couples.
- You have no long-term plans.
- You take separate vacations.
- You buy a car, house, pet without consulting the other person.

- You're never there when he/she calls.
- You don't return your date's phone calls.
- You get a post office box.
- Your date moved, neglected to inform you, and didn't leave a forwarding address.
- You have your number changed and don't tell.
- A love child has been left on your front porch.

Chapter 5

. . . .

Catch Phrases

General Catch Phrases and How to Interpret Them

I love you; I'm just not in love with you.
Translation:
I've called the lawyer.
I have a lover.
You're toast.
Color me gone.
Can't we just be friends?
Translation:
There's no chemistry.

I'd rather die than kiss you.
I feel really guilty about doing
you wrong, so I'd like to pre-
tend you don't hate me to ease
my conscience.
I'm seeing someone else.
I don't want to have to find my
own place.
I'd like to borrow money.
Will you take care of my dog?
You're too good for me
(basically the same as
"I love you; I'm just not
in love with you").

Translation:
I'm outta here.
Crying, begging, pleading,
and threatening won't do you
any good.
I'm going to treat you badly.

**Can we cuddle and not
have sex?**

Translation:

If a woman says it:
I haven't made up my mind
about you.
If you make a pass, you're
scum.

If you don't make a pass,
you're gay.

If a man says it:

I think I'm too drunk to
perform.

I'm going to seduce you.

Can I just come up and use
your bathroom?

Translation:

I plan to seduce you nearly
immediately.

I want to spend the night.

I have a bathroom fetish.

My mom would love you.

Translation:

I hate you.

I really want to get married.

My dad will hate you.

My mom is dead.

I want to have sex with you.

Will you cook for me?

You're just like my ex.

Translation:

You're history.

I hate you.

We've just had a huge fight.

You deserve someone better than me (a more urgent,

**virulent form of "You're
too good").**
Translation:
*I've done something awful,
and you're going to find out.
I'm already seeing someone else.*

Believe in fate.
Translation:
*I'm seeing someone else.
I've decided to go back to
my ex.
I'm leaving for a three-year trip,
and I'd like you to be faithful
although I'm not going to be.*

We're soul mates.
Translation:
If a man says it:
I want sex.
I want to go back to my ex.
If a woman says it:
I want to get married.
You'd love my friend.
Translation:
I'm passing you on.
We have nothing in common.
I'm furious with my friend
and hate you.
Do what you think is best.

Translation:

You're about to do something
I hate, and I'll never forget it
and punish you forever.
I have a graduate degree in guilt.
Do what I want . . . now.
Don't you dare.

I've never felt this way before.

Translation:

Here we go again.
Let's have sex.
You're standing on my bunion.

I thought I'd just stay in tonight.

Translation:
I have a date.
You have a herpes sore I don't want.
I got a better offer.
There's a party I don't want to invite you to.

We should get together sometime.

Translation:
I'm seeing someone, but it's not going well.
I'm passive. Ask me out and pay for the date and I'll go.

I wouldn't go out with you if you were the last person on the planet.

By now, you've digested the material and are a dating expert in the making. You've done the work. Good job!